MYTHS & MS.

AN INTER-GENERATIONAL PLAY
ABOUT REINCARNATION AND ABORTION

ROSIE ROSENZWEIG

ANAPHORA LITERARY PRESS

BROWNSVILLE, TEXAS

ANAPHORA LITERARY PRESS
1898 Athens Street
Brownsville, TX 78520
https://anaphoraliterary.com

Book design by Anna Faktorovich, Ph.D.

Printed in the United States of America, United Kingdom and in Australia on acid-free paper.

Author Photo by Lora Brody
Edited by Shauneice Robinson

Published in 2018 by Anaphora Literary Press

Myths & Ms.: An Inter-generational Play about Reincarnation and Abortion
Rosie Rosenzweig—1st edition.

Library of Congress Control Number: 2017954173

Library Cataloging Information
Rosenzweig, Rosie, 1937-, author.
    Myths & Ms. / Rosie Rosenzweig
    102 p. ; 9 in.
    ISBN 978-1-68114-382-8 (softcover : alk. paper)
    ISBN 978-1-68114-383-5 (hardcover : alk. paper)
    ISBN 978-1-68114-384-2 (e-book)
1. Performing Arts—Theater—Playwriting.
2. Drama—Religious & Liturgical.
3. Social Science—Abortion & Birth Control.
PN3035: The Jewish theater
812: American drama in English

MYTHS & MS.

AN INTER-GENERATIONAL PLAY ABOUT REINCARNATION AND ABORTION

ROSIE ROSENZWEIG

For Ronn Smith, Director/Dramaturg par excellence,

without whom this play would have never been completed.

And Annette Miller of Shakespeare & Co.,

For whom the role of Ruth was written,

For your support from the beginning a decade ago.

CONTENTS

Cast of Characters

* **Jack**   A Civil Rights Lawyer .
* **Ruth**   Jack's middle-aged wife.
* **Chayya**   Spirit of Ruth's Immigrant Mother.
* **Judith**   Jack & Ruth's daughter; A counsellor.
* **Henry**   Judith's lover.
* **Tamar**   Judith's daughter; An art student with a slight stutter.
* **Josh**   Tamar's friend.

* **Additional Voices:** Radio Host Nick Davis Voice, Woman's
                  Voice, Operator's Voice, Melissa French's Voice,
                  Woman Call-in Voice, Priscilla's Voice, and
                  Judith's Therapist's Voice.

PREQUEL

Darkened stage slowly lights up to reveal a coffin with a rabbi chanting Hebrew Psalms.

A door opens allowing a sliver of light into the room.
Ruth peeks in tentatively followed by a rabbi at her elbow who guides her to the coffin. They approach the coffin. He opens the lid and Ruth's astonished face reflects a muted light.

The lid is lowered, pall bearers enter, and carry the coffin to a grave surrounded by mourners as it is lowered.

Kaddish begins and the mourners include Ruth, daughter of the deceased, Judith, and bewildered Tamar. They seat themselves on boxes as the Kaddish continues for a time. Ruth eyes Judith with concern. Tamar, unseen by Judith, comes behind her grandmother Ruth, and whispers in her ear.

After the Kaddish, guests silently comfort the mourners and leave.
Judith and Tamar exit. Ruth rises, finds her luggage, and exits.

BLACKOUT

ACT 1: SCENE 1

RUTH'S LIVING ROOM, BROOKLINE, MASSACHUSETTS

Ruth enters wheeling luggage, and turns on a light. She finds a sheet, and places it over a mirror. She nods to a portrait of Chayya, lights a large candle, hangs up her coat, and exits. The ghost of Chayya appears, observing all.

Jack enters, turns on the radio, and notices her luggage. He carelessly knocks off the sheet over the mirror, as he searches for paper and a pen. He listens to pro-life and pro-choice voices on an NPR talk show. The voice of talk show host Nick Davis emerges with:

Nick Davis

This is the Nick Davis Show. With interviews and call-ins from our listeners, we examine the important issues that confront America. Today is the 30th anniversary of the Supreme Court decision legalizing abortion that has polarized our nation with debate and even violence. In regard to Roe v. Wade, has America changed within the last 30 years? This is Nick Davis Introducing anti-abortionist author Melissa Anderson…

JACK:

Super-imposed
Ruth, are you finally back?
Ruthie?
Where did you put the paper?

RUTH:

Offstage
What do you need paper for?
We're not supposed to write today.

JACK:

I'm exempt; I'm the son in-law.
Remember! I don't have to mourn.
Oh, I found it.

RUTH:

Entering.
Already you want me to find something?

JACK:

Ruthie please, I REALLY have to listen to this broadcast.

RUTH:

Something happened in the airport. It was so upsetting, especially
after burying Mama.

Ruth makes eye contact with her mother in the portrait.

JACK:

Super-imposed. In a falsetto voice.
Well, hello to you Jack and how did *YOU* manage in my absence?
Returning to his normal voice.
I ran out of the food that you left me.

RUTH:

Pizza! You could order a pizza. You always manage.

JACK:

Barely.

RUTH:

You could have come with us. There was plenty of food.
I'm sure you managed to get that important work done,
write your arguments, attend those meetings, or even catch a couple
of demonstrations.

JACK:

Demonstrations. You used to love them.
Remember the sex after the March on Washington?

RUTH:

Then, it was August.
We could sleep on the grass.
Now it's dangerous.
Today you can't carry a little Judith on your shoulders.

JACK:

It was exciting for her… and it was a family outing then.

RUTH:

Now, why don't you tell that to her?
How long are you going to stay mad!
> *Noticing that the sheet has fallen exposing the mirror, RUTH*
> *picks up the sheet, and holds it while gazing at her mother.*
Ach! Go listen to your program.

JACK:

> *Picks up one corner of the sheet.*
I'm really, really sorry for your loss,
but Ruthie, do I have to tell you how much this means to me?
You know I love getting my "two cents" in.
This is about Roe V. Wade on NPR. Come on Ruthie.
> *Playfully he drapes the sheet around her.*
She's talking about killing babies!!

RUTH:

We had our own Roe V. Wade didn't we Jack?

JACK:

Again with that?

RUTH:

My mother would have loved that baby!
But I didn't have the nerve to tell her.

JACK:

Listen kid, that happened a long time ago, even before Judith.

RUTH:

Jack, did you want me to abort because you liked Julie, another leftie like you?

JACK:

Wow. That's a new one.
Ruthie, I'm here now.
    Ruth rummages through another drawer.
What are you looking for?

RUTH:

Pictures. Me with my mother when I was Tamar's age.
Her holding Judith as a baby. Did you throw them away?

JACK:

I'd never throw those away.

RUTH:

You threw away plenty after the great reveal.
Love does strange things to people.

JACK:

She can't be in love with him!
You're dreaming!

RUTH:

Yes, I do dream Jack. A lot. Usually it's a little boy.
Last night there was no boy.
Jack, last night my mother came to me.

JACK:

How can that be? She's dead. You just buried her.

RUTH:

You are so literal!

JACK:

Hello, I'm a lawyer!
And you, you're such a dreamer!

RUTH:

"A dream unattended is like an unopened letter."

JACK:

Are you quoting those rabbis again?

RUTH:

Without the logic of the rabbis and their Talmud,
YOU, my dear husband, would be without a profession.

JACK:

I don't know when to take you seriously.
THIS
   Points at the radio
is serious!

RUTH:

Do you want something to eat?

JACK:

No. Why would I want something to eat now?
   Pause
Okay, now I know it's serious.

RUTH:

My mother's trying to talk to me and I know it.

JACK:

So, talk to her.

RUTH:

It's not about talking back. She wants to tell me something.
That's what the dream was about.

JACK:

So, listen to her.

RUTH:

Jack, in my dream, my mother was shining.
She was filled with a bright light.

JACK:

Can't you just move on?

RUTH:

Jack, she just died!
I'm between two worlds.
You listen to the talk show, I light a candle for my mother.
I light Sabbath candles and you blow them out.

JACK:

I just don't want to go through any of this
        Sarcastically
"spiritualistic" stuff right now.

RUTH:

Spiritualistic?

JACK:

Or whatever you call it!
Can I just listen to "The Connection?"
My favorite talk show.

RUTH:

But this is a critical time.
The soul is confused after death.
That's why we place sheets on the mirrors.

JACK:

Isn't that so we won't vainly think about how we look?

RUTH:

BUT, this *is* the time to think about what the loss means to us.
And you, you're supposed to listen to me, the mourner.
You should be the comforter.
You're supposed to bring me food, take care of me.

JACK:

I always try to…

RUTH:

Super-imposed
Try! This is not supposed to be an effort.
You should understand loss.

JACK:

I never really know what you want from me.

RUTH:

I don't. want. to listen. to a talk show! I want quiet.
Can't you just be quiet and not always talk about what YOU need?
When your father died, I just waited for you to talk.

JACK:

I waited for you to say something funny to make me smile.

RUTH:

Funny? Jokes are not appropriate in a house of mourning.

JACK:

I could have used something funny.

RUTH:

To escape the sorrow?
I don't want to run away from what my mother meant to me.

JACK:

I didn't want to deal with—all this.

RUTH:

What "this?"

JACK:

The candles, the sheet on the mirrors…
He holds the sheet up to her.

RUTH:

There's a dignity in acknowledging loss.

JACK:

I don't know how to do this.

RUTH:

That's honest.
That's really good.

JACK:

What? Rating me again?
Are you my therapist now?

RUTH:

When you can say to me, "Look, I can't deal with it,"
at least I can deal with that.
This isn't a therapy thing; it's real life talking.

JACK:

You can deal with me not dealing?

RUTH:

Yes, when you tell me your honest feelings.
Just put your cards on the table.

JACK:

We're playing cards now? "Texas hold-em?"
Any wild cards?

RUTH:

This isn't funny. I won't laugh!

JACK:

Okay, I won't laugh either.

RUTH:

But when you snuff out my candles, and say,

"I don't know what's become of you."
I can't be with you.

JACK:

I'm sorry about the candles.
I really don't know how to deal with the mirrors.
I like to know how I look before I go out.

RUTH:

You look great.

JACK:

Why doesn't Chayya want to look in the mirror to see
how she looks? She was so vain about her looks.

RUTH:

She can't see how she looks. She has no body.
She looks in the mirror and sees nothing.

JACK:

You are losing me.
I've never looked in the mirror and seen nothing.

RUTH:

Because you are in a body! You're very materialistic, dear.

JACK:

Me? The pro-bono champion of the underdog?

RUTH:

Political materialism!

JACK:

What is political materialism?

RUTH:

Accruing good causes like money in the bank.
It's just another form of materialism.

JACK:

You just made that up, didn't you?
Oh, let's talk about your memories.

RUTH:

You're supposed to shut up and wait for me to come up with it.

JACK:

So, come up with something.

RUTH:

Oh great. Can't you just shut up? Shut up! Shut up!
Please. Just hold my hand.

JACK:

> *Resigned*

Like this?

> *Pause*

RUTH:

I don't know if I ever told you this story about my mother.

JACK:

Yeah?

RUTH:

It makes me believe in, well, something more.
I never told it to anyone before.

JACK:

What?

RUTH;

You *can* be cute when I catch you off guard.

JACK:

So, tell me already.

RUTH:

My mother glowed. She glowed in the dark.
Don't look at me like that. Her friends all told me these stories.
My father said that she glowed around the campfire
at Emma Goldman's commune in New Jersey.

JACK:

I'd glow in the dark around Emma Goldman too.
Remember? They all condemned Castro after he won the Cuban revolution:
"What kind of revolution is this? There's still going to be a government.
What kind of anarchist is he?"

RUTH:

Those stories you knew, but the glowing?
Her final days at hospice, I had to tell her she could go,
that it was all right to go.
Then she shouted over and over again:
"BUT I haven't done it yet!!"

JACK:

She did plenty.
She was a divorced immigrant woman.
She bravely left an arranged marriage, came to America, found love,
helped organize the garment workers' union, *and* she raised you.

RUTH:

You just don't get it, do you?

JACK:

What's to get?
She's dead!

RUTH:

Jack, it's just like that movie: "Groundhog Day."

JACK:

"Groundhog Day????"
    Scoffs.
What does a wild animal have to do with her life?

RUTH:

Remember that movie with Bill Murray?
He kept dying again and again; then waking up to the same day.
Repeatedly.
He has to figure out how to make the most of that new day,
or metaphorically, each new life.

JACK:

This is not logical.

RUTH:

No, it's "spiritualistic!"
Ma knew she was dying; she was hysterical about it.
She knew that she hadn't done the job in this lifetime.
The doctors, they were only concerned with the physical pain.
Finally, one came and said, "The suffering had to end."
The rabbis had already brought in the witnesses.

JACK:

Witnesses?

RUTH:

People to comfort her with Psalms.
The body is not left alone until it is buried in the ground.

JACK:

Enough. Enough.

RUTH:

I had to identify her body.
I picked up the coffin lid—the room was full of light!

JACK:

This story is giving me the creeps. I like the other story better about

your mother
locking the door to her room in the old age home. Because she had a lover!

RUTH:
Oh, that one! Are you sure you don't want something to eat?

JACK:
No.
Just finish that airport story. This has got to be better.

RUTH:
I should call Judith.

JACK:
Annoyed.
Judith again?
Please tell the story.

RUTH:
So you were listening...
This man with his expensive suit talks loudly into his cell phone;
 he's bragging about his boat.

JACK:
Did he have a trophy wife with him? I bet she was some looker.

RUTH:
You break my heart again and again. He was alone.

JACK:
Give a guy a break. So, what did this shallow materialist say?

RUTH:
Offered a nice price for his boat, he said that he'd sooner "sell his children."

JACK:
This is going to be good, I think.

RUTH:

I say: "You'd sooner sell your children?" Pulls out this photo and says, "but you have to see this boat."
I said, "I don't have to see the boat, I see who you are."

JACK:

And, like your mother who sacrificed her life for you, you said…

RUTH:

"Shame on you. What if your children heard you say that?"
He claimed to be having "a private conversation." So, I said:
"Excuse me young man, you were shouting.
Face the wall if you want private!"
He dropped his glasses and ran to board his plane.

JACK:

You take no prisoners. Just like your mother.

RUTH:

I hope so.
        Dismissively fanning him off with the back of her hand.
Now go listen to your program. It's time to call Judith.

JACK:

You can't go a day without calling her?

RUTH:

If you weren't so stubborn you would call her too.
You're the one she needs to talk to; maybe that's why…

Jack petulantly turns the radio louder. The announcer asks for call-ins.
Ruth talks into her cell phone, while Jack picks up the landline.
Ruth hangs up, while Jack dials and waits.

RUTH:

You know, that child still comes to me in my dreams?

JACK:

Please I can't talk to you right now. I'm on the phone.

WOMAN'S VOICE:

Abortion is an unjust act that harms women who abort. We have mounting evidence of the physical and psychological devastation that follow abortion.
We have to advocate not only for the unborn child but also for unrequited motherhood!!

A car horn honks. Ruth puts on her coat, and finds her suitcase.

RUTH:

I should go. It's the car service.
  Exits slowly.

OPERATOR'S VOICE:

Jack from Brookline, you're on the air. Please turn down the volume on your radio.

BLACKOUT

ACT 1: SCENE 2

SETTING: JUDITH'S KITCHEN. CAMBRIDGE, MASSACHUSETTS

Judith enters with her arms full of groceries. After placing her load on the counter, she turns on the radio to hear the NICK DAVIS Show. She sits down, and rubs her stomach.

NICK DAVIS Voice:
We have some callers on the line waiting to talk to Melissa French, author of *Pro-life for the 21st century.* A while back we heard from Jack from Brookline…

JUDITH:
Dad?

NICK DAVIS' VOICE:
…who was politically active during the days of illegal abortions. He described how he helped his girlfriend find an abortionist.

JUDITH:
Mom?

NICK DAVIS' VOICE:
Quite a difficult task in those days.
He even quoted Sarah Weddington who won the Roe V. Wade decision.
Says he was her law clerk.

MELISSA FRENCH's VOICE:
I covered her in Chapter 8 of my book.
Jack is a poor deluded man to help his fiancée abort.
Imagine what that baby would be like today!
He called it just a bunch of cells.

NICK DAVIS' VOICE:

We have another caller. It's Priscilla from Texas. Go ahead Priscilla.

PRISCILLA'S VOICE:

I agree so much with Miss French and all y'all about killing children…

JUDITH:

This isn't a child yet!

PRISCILLA:

I have six children and obviously, I've been pro-life and my church…

Tamar enters with ear pods in her ear, dancing, rapping, and repeating the refrain. Her hands are hennaed.

TAMAR

I have to be who I wanna be!
I got to do what I got to do!
I got to see what I got to see!
I got to be WHO
I wanna be!
Rings in my nose,
in my ears, on my toes,
Purple is my hair,
Here, there, and everywhere."

JUDITH:

I'm pro-life too, you bitch. What about my life? What about Tamar's life?

TAMAR:

M-m-mom, what's up? Why are you yelling my name at the radio?

JUDITH:

This is my dad's favorite program. AND he was just talking on this show.

TAMAR:

Grandpa's not talking to you because of your new boyfriend,
But—but, but—he's talking in public on the radio?
I go away for one semester, come home –and- and UNCLE HENRY
(?) is living in my house???? Grandpa's friend? With an earring in his
ear?

JUDITH:

I'm just trying…

TAMAR:

Tr-trying. Did you ever think about what- what this does to my life?
I don't need two grandfathers. It's weird.

JUDITH:

Give me a break kid. My grandmother just died and my father won't
             talk to me.
Every day after school, she would always call me to say:
"'*Zeese Meydl*'—sweet girl. Did you ask a good question today?"

TAMAR:

I can really re-relate to that!

JUDITH:

Help me find that music you listen to.
I'm trying to get into the head of a pregnant teenage client I saw
today.

TAMAR:

That's why you're looking for my music?
If you really want to know my music, you have to move to it. Like
this…

>   *Dancing, Tamar pulls Judith up from the chair and moves her
> to dance.*
>   *Chayya enters, and begins to dance as her face assumes more
> color.*

TAMAR:

What's—what's—got you so messed up? Are you throwing up again?

JUDITH:

This call-in show has a pro-life witch carrying on...

TAMAR:

Just what you need at the end of the day.

JUDITH:

This teenager who is cutting, burning herself, with knives, with
 lighted cigarettes.
She has rings in her... her...
Hey, did you just get a new ring in your nose?
What happens if you catch a cold with that ring in your nose?

TAMAR:

W-wait until you see the new tattoo.
There's a new one in my boob.
 It really gives me a charge whenever I move. Wanna see?

JUDITH:

Tamar!!!

TAMAR:

Hah! Got you!
I won't get a boob ring 'cause—'cause after seeing you and grandma.
I knew a boob ring would make me too
                    saggy...

JUDITH:

I need to hug you.
                    Pause
Did you see your therapist today?

TAMAR:

I don't...
I really DON'T want to talk about it.
That's confidential, remember?

JUDITH:

I'm sorry. I'm sorry.
>   *Pause.*
Any new paintings?

TAMAR:

Well, uh, well I did… Just one good piece. It's about grandma.

JUDITH:

I'd like to see it.
Maybe later?

TAMAR:

Yeah. Sure.

JUDITH:

Hey, can you help me unpack these? I've got your favorite stuff here.

TAMAR:

No problem.
>   *Unpacking groceries*
What's this? This doesn't look good.

JUDITH:

Your hair looks different;
did you do another color?

TAMAR:

Yeah.

JUDITH:

Hey…oh. Wow.

TAMAR:

Do you like it?

JUDITH:

I like purple but I liked the color from last week.

Why change?

TAMAR:

I feel purple today.

JUDITH:

I need to sit down.
I'm a little tired.

TAMAR:

You're always tired.

JUDITH:

It was a long day today.
It's probably the flu that's going around. Wait. Your eyes look
          bloodshot.

TAMAR:

Yeah, I don't feel so good either. I was up late and...

JUDITH:

 Hey, look under the counter. Let's have a lavender footbath tonight.
Maybe we could soak and watch TV tonight?

TAMAR:

Um, I don't know...

JUDITH:

Let's watch "The Bachelor."
We could eat popcorn, veg out together and not fight?
     Retching.
It must be the popcorn idea...

TAMAR:

Were you sick again this morning?

JUDITH:

Mentioning popcorn was not a good idea.
Everybody at the agency has this flu thing.

I didn't sleep very well.

TAMAR:

Ma, you've been throwing up for weeks.

JUDITH:

Are you worried about me?

TAMAR:

Yeah, a little.

JUDITH:

That's sweet.
> *Henry enters.*
> *Tamar moves away.*

HENRY:

Maybe the 50 minute hour should be shortened to 10 minutes. Oh.
Tamar…

JUDITH:

We might have a girls' night tonight.
I think we're just going to kind of cozy up together, just the two of us.

HENRY:

Where do I fit into this?

JUDITH:

Don't you have some insurance claims to file tonight?

HENRY:

Yeah, but that can wait.

TAMAR:

We're just watching TV. You're not missing anything.

JUDITH:

Well, what do you think about him joining us?

TAMAR:

I thought- I thought, that—that it would be just us—that footbath
                    thing,
Watch TV, and maybe color your hair like mine tonight?

HENRY:

Tamar. I feel weird about me here too… Shouldn't we talk…

TAMAR:

I'm, I'm just going to chill, do my homework. I'll—I'll see you later.
        Tamar exits.

JUDITH:

Are you sure?
        Calling to Tamar who is offstage
Then I'll just talk to Henry for a bit. I'll come up in five minutes.
OK?
        Turning to face Henry
I just don't know what color her hair's going to be tomorrow.

HENRY:

I kind of like the hair thing.
        Judith begins to move towards him.
I thought there were house rules:
Not while Tamar's around.

JUDITH:

We could break the rules.
Like Tamar tries to do sometimes.

HENRY:

I'm feeling uncomfortable now.

JUDITH:

You get me pregnant and now you're uncomfortable!
Thank you very much!

HENRY:

Judith remember this was your idea; *you* suggested I move in.
You know… you could easily have an abortion at the clinic.

JUDITH:

But this baby could do great things in the world.
We could home school it to…

HENRY:

To go to protests like Jack?
Is this you talking or your father?
A kid should be allowed to follow his own path,
not walk the road his parents force him to walk!

JUDITH:

Raising a global citizen to take political action…

HENRY:

What if the child wants to be an artist like Tamar?
Picasso did more for peace with Guernica than all the protestors in
the world.

JUDITH:

But my father…

HENRY:

Your father is an ardent liberal, sometimes too ardent…

JUDITH:

What does that mean?

HENRY:

He brought you up to follow him. This cost me our friendship.
You know very well I distance myself from politics.
We've talked about this before. My work is my politics.
Judith please, I have other children.

JUDITH:

So, I did come on to you. I like touching you…
She moves closer to him. Over time, they get more affectionate

and eventually have a long embrace.

The ghost of Chayya comes out of the shadows, observes, and then withdraws.

HENRY:

Sometimes you just don't get me. It's OK to have differences.
> *Pause.*
Judith are you using me?

JUDITH:

> *Laughing until her eyes tear.*
The feminists would love this...

HENRY:

Come on Judith.
You are almost my daughter's age.

JUDITH:

Does that turn you on?
A younger woman?
Well I love having a boy toy.
> *Laughing again*

HENRY:

Well I AM flattered. You may have saved me from a mid-life crisis.
> *Pause.*
Seriously, am I your last chance to...

JUDITH:

Don't go there.

HENRY:

> *Super-imposed*
Am I just another cause?
> *Points to her stomach*
Do you want to be left with another fatherless child?

JUDITH:

Are you threatening…

HENRY:

We never talked marriage.
Judith, I'm a responsible man.

JUDITH:

First, you get turned on then, you become full of startling insights…

HENRY:

Hello? I'm the psychiatrist. Remember?
On that note, what are we doing in this relationship, this office romance?
>   *Turns away to calm down.*

JUDITH:

>   *Long silence.*
I have to get dinner.

HENRY:

I need some air.
>   *Reaches for his jacket.*

JUDITH:

Where are you going?

A knocking at the door that began earlier becomes audible. Henry opens the door to find Ruth with a shopping bag of groceries and her luggage.

HENRY:

How long have you been there?

RUTH:

I knocked and knocked.
>   *Henry takes her packages.*

HENRY:

I'm so glad you came.

I hope you're not angry with me for…

RUTH:

I didn't bring this on myself, but if it was me who found you in bed together…
Henry, I'm not Jack. I get this; you were the go-to guy for women who needed…

HENRY:

Someone to listen to them. Like you Ruth.
Back then, you knew I would become a psychiatrist.
You told me so, very often.

RUTH:

Oh yeah, you were so shy and so safe, such a perfect confidant.
Jack and I had our worst fights then.

HENRY:

And now?

RUTH:

That's not why I am here.
        Turning to Judith.
Judith, don't you remember when you were in high school and your friend left his size 14 sneakers at the door?
I slammed doors loudly and went into the basement singing at the top of my lungs?

JUDITH:

Mom enough of that!
        Looking at the extra bags of groceries.
I just went grocery shopping!

RUTH:

Judith, you got off the phone too fast. I knew something was wrong.

JUDITH:

Look, I don't have time to chat. I have to make dinner.
You couldn't call before you traveled here?

RUTH:

I brought you dinner.

JUDITH:

Still trying to reach me through food?

RUTH:

What else do I have? Do we talk?
The least I can do is cook for you.

HENRY:

Ruth, that works for me. Let me help you.
> *Takes her luggage.*
> *Ruth walks in and trips over the foot bath.*

RUTH:

Oiy! Oiy! What is this?
> *Holds onto the table while rubbing her stubbed toe.*

JUDITH:

That is a foot bath. It's a little Jacuzzi for feet.
> *Tamar peeks in.*

RUTH:

A foot bath?
> *Lifts it up and puts her finger in one of the jet-spray outlets.*
I remember getting my Mama a *shisel,*

JUDITH:

A what?

RUTH:

A *shisel,* a little pan full of water.
It was my job to take her shoes off when she came home from the
        sweatshop.
I was so small that her shoes were as big my forearm.
She used to sing when I helped her.

JUDITH:

Bubby Chayya? Then it must be in my genes, I love a foot bath after work.

RUTH:

Judith, you look tired and pale.

JUDITH:

It's just the flu Ma.

RUTH:

Let me do the dinner and you rest.
Then you won't be mad at me anymore.

HENRY:

I'm not mad at you!
What did you bring?
Nothing with sugar I hope…

TAMAR:

Entering.
Grandma! You-you came!

RUTH:

Shhhush!!

TAMAR:

Mom, can Grandma stay over in my room?

RUTH:

Is that all right?

JUDITH:

I'm too tired to object.
Tamar, help Grandma with her stuff.

HENRY:

I'll unpack the food.
I just want to be careful about sugar.

Peruses the food labels as he unpacks it.

Tamar and Ruth exit deep in conversation.

JUDITH:

Not going out anymore dear?

HENRY:

I really like your mother.
    Whispering.
You haven't told her yet, have you.

JUDITH:

Dad would never show up unannounced.
She became so strange at the funeral, so into her new books.

HENRY:

Huh. I just read that the Dalai Lama said that there just might even be
unfinished business from the last lifetime.

JUDITH:

Knock it off! I feel as tired as my Bubby must have been at the end of the day.
My feet really ache.
    Henry dutifully rubs her feet in silence.
She always knew when I was lying. The night I lost my virginity, I came home so late.
She knew I was lying.

HENRY:

Are you lying now?

JUDITH:

I'm not telling my mother about this. That's not lying.
She knew when Dad was lying, especially after his ill-timed travels.
I wonder what he lied about?

HENRY:

Stop your erotic fantasies.
This is getting weird again.

JUDITH:

My only erotic fantasies are about you babe.

HENRY:

You have me right here, you made sure of that.

JUDITH:

Do I really have you?

Henry exits with a disgruntled expression on his face.

BLACKOUT

ACT 1: SCENE 3

TAMAR'S BEDROOM
TAMAR and RUTH

TAMAR:

Grandma, you can sleep on my futon and I'll sleep on the floor mat.

RUTH:

I won't bump into you at night, will I?

TAMAR:

I'll put it on the other side of my room. It'll be like camping out.

RUTH:

With my aging bladder, I get up more than you do.
>*They both laugh.*

TAMAR:

You won't tell Mom that I asked you to come over, will you?

RUTH:

Have I ever told your mother anything you've told me?
>*She looks around.*

Is this a new look?

TAMAR:

Those, those are my new paintings—a new series.
I had to paint, um, portraits of people, of my family, and friends.

RUTH:

Am I here?

TAMAR:

Um, I'm working on you.

Shyly shows her the sketch.

RUTH:

I just see a golden color, no face.
You're so talented—just like my mother.
She was so gifted; she could draw, and she could sing...

TAMAR:

I did it from an old picture of you.

RUTH:

And where are the eyes?

TAMAR:

Well, that's-that's sort of abstract.

RUTH:

Isn't that what you call magenta? It's a royal color.

TAMAR:

I was trying to do blues I guess. I've been painting with blues lately.

RUTH:

Picasso did have a blue period.

TAMAR:

How do you know that?

RUTH:

I'm a docent at the museum. What is blue to you?

TAMAR:

I don't know. I—it's a good color to work with.
I read that Van Gogh, toward the end of his life, used only red.
I thought it would be interesting to use only one color.

RUTH:

Just don't cut your ear off.
You have a lot of rings there in your ear.

Just how many have you got?

TAMAR:

Ahh…um three in this ear. Four in this other ear.

RUTH:

I never let your mother pierce her ears. Want to ask me why?

TAMAR:

Sure Grandma. So why did-did you never let my mother…

RUTH:

What are you, a comedienne?
A straight man we used to call it.
OK.
During biblical times,
slaves had to be set free after seven years of service.
Bu-ut if a slave wanted to stay on with the master;
his ear would be placed on the doorpost.

TAMAR:

And now, why did the slave put his ear on the doorpost?

RUTH:

So a dowel could be hammered into the lobe to make a hole, just like
yours.

TAMAR:

Ewwwwww!

RUTH:

So, everyone knew that a slave with a ring in his ear was always a slave
by choice.
I believe pierced ears mean someone's a slave to fashion.
    They laugh.
End of lecture.

TAMAR:

You did notice that my mom has pierced ears now?

RUTH:

That was inevitable.
So, what will you do when you leave home?
I see your hair is purple today.

TAMAR:

Do you like it?

RUTH:

Purple is close to magenta.
I really want to know why purple?

TAMAR:

It's my favorite color.
Today. It's bright but it's not like too...

RUTH:

Brassy?

TAMAR:

It'll fade a little after I wash it more.

RUTH:

With your long skirt, you look like a religious young woman.

TAMAR:

I'm definitely not religious.

RUTH:

So, how many Jews are there at your art school?

TAMAR:

I don't know. Why is it so important to be Jewish anyway?
I'd rather be Buddhist; Buddhists are much more quiet.

RUTH:

You think Jews don't meditate?
    Pulls the book "Jewish Meditation & Reincarnation" out of her

bag.

TAMAR:

Jews meditate?
> *Flips through the pages of the book, and stops at one page.*

What's this about dreams?   I thought you didn't like to interpret
> dreams.

Mom says you were always against her therapists interpreting her
> dreams.

RUTH:

I'm not against facing your flaws and changing.

I am against therapists blaming mothers for all that's wrong in
> people's lives,

to prove blame. This book says that some dreams are hidden mystical
> messages,

like unopened letters.

TAMAR:

Mystical messages?

RUTH:

This Rabbi was called the Ba'al Shem Tov, "Master of the Good
> Name."

His soul travelled in his sleep to other worlds to find these messages
and right wrongs.

TAMAR:

No one, no -one can do that, can they?
> *Holding back tears.*

RUTH:

What? Tamar. Darling.
> *Cradles Tamar for a time, and then hums a lullaby.*

RUTH:

Remember how I used to sing this to you when you were a little girl?

TAMAR:

I remember getting up at night to crawl under your covers when I
slept over.
I'd be so scared.
Sometimes I dream about that.
I have funny dreams.

RUTH:

Dreams? Like what?

TAMAR:

An old woman dressed in old-fashioned clothes.
She keeps holding out her arms to me.
> *Chayya imitates the stance holding out her arms from the*
shadows.

RUTH:

That doesn't sound so scary.

TAMAR:

Well she sort of looks like you, only different and older.

RUTH:

Grandmothers do watch over the family. Remember "Fiddler on the
Roof?"

TAMAR:

Even I knew that wasn't real. Tevya made that dream up!
> *They laugh and pause.*
This grandmother, the-the one in my dream, sings and turns into a
baby.

RUTH:

One Rabbi believes that some of the Jews who perished in the
                    Holocaust
have been reborn in Brooklyn, so that they can continue their soul
                    work.

TAMAR:

Soul work?

RUTH:

Each reincarnation works to fulfill what the spirit wasn't able to do in
the last lifetime.

TAMAR:

Picks up her art work and adds some color to Ruth's portrait.
Do you think your mother ever wanted to be an artist?

RUTH:

She was always crocheting and making flower arrangements.
Being artistic in everything, even the house arrangements.
And singing… Always singing.

TAMAR:

Well maybe I take after her. Here it's finished.

RUTH:

Looks like my mother.
Weeping silently

TAMAR:

Oh Grandma, you really miss her? I'm so sorry she died.

RUTH:

Me too. Poor Ma. She wasn't allowed to sing in the old country.
She ran away from a bad marriage after her first baby died in
childbirth.
She hoped to sing in America. That didn't happen.

TAMAR:

Why not?

RUTH:

She had to make a living so she sewed clothes. She sang the union
songs though.
When she got sick, her voice just gave out.

Stares blankly into the distance for some time.
Ah! This is a wonderful piece you made here.
She studies it.
Tell me, do you feel better at this new school?

TAMAR:

Sometimes. I still don't really like school, but I do like the art classes.

RUTH:

Looks at Tamar's hennaed hands.
Does everyone do art on their hands at this school?

TAMAR:

Not everyone. I got into this art history class on body painting, so I
thought I would try it.
Oh, um, don't tell Mom that these aren't real tattoos.
They both chuckle.

RUTH:

Have you ever seen the Ethiopian Jews, the Falashas, and their art?

TAMAR:

No, but Josh studied them. He helped me draw on my hands.

RUTH:

Josh? Do you like him?

TAMAR:

He is an artist like me: visual, musical.
Mom goes crazy if we talk about art too much around her.
Almost as crazy as when I ask her about my father.

RUTH:

She was really hurt. Maybe it's best to give her space and time.
You know about needing that, right?
Pause.
Do the kids in your school have tattoos?

TAMAR:

A lot of them do, but, but I do know one girl who um, did her own tattoo.

RUTH:

Ouch!

TAMAR:

Yeah, it was sort of a mess. I didn't really like it.

RUTH:

But do you really want one?

TAMAR:

I haven't come up with a design I want.

RUTH:

Just take a look at my skin.
All these veins.
Can you imagine a tattoo on your skin when you're older?
My grandmother had a tattoo on her arm with numbers...

TAMAR:

Doctors know how to get them off now.

RUTH:

They can erase the numbers, but not the memories.
So, what would your own design do for you?

TAMAR:

That's the same question that Dr. Chapman asks me.

RUTH:

Who's Dr. Chapman?

TAMAR:

Mom made me go to a therapist for my stuttering.
I-I don't like talking to strangers.
But-but, but it's required for this new school.

Now I really like her a lot.
I really do.

RUTH:

What do you like about her?

TAMAR:

She listens to me.
She suggests something for me to say in troublesome situations.
She doesn't tell me what to do.

RUTH:

Do I tell you what to do?

TAMAR:

Never, but Mom does and Henry, our resident shrink, is full of
                  insights.
They can't keep anything to themselves.
With Dr. Chapman, it's *all* confidential,
but I still like talking to you better, Grandma.

RUTH:

I'm so glad. Did you tell her about Mom and all your worries?

TAMAR:

That's why I called you. It's really weird here. Sometimes, I, uh, I, ah,
                  sometimes…
they really freak me out…

RUTH:

Shah. Shah. SHHH.
                  Embraces her

TAMAR:

I—I just, ah…

RUTH:

Ok, you don't have to tell me, but you DO talk to her about what's
                  wrong?

TAMAR:

Yeah, yeah…

RUTH:

Boys?

TAMAR:

Ah, well, ah, I don't know…she—
 Stammers.
Well there is Josh.

RUTH:

Talk to him; talk to her; talk to anyone you want, just as long as you
talk to someone.

TAMAR:

Grandma, you're too much for me right now.
 Short silence.

RUTH:

Is there anything more about this Dr. Chapman?

TAMAR:

She's not uptight. Once she wore two different black shoes.
Oh yeah, I heard someone call her the Big "I".

RUTH:

"Big I", what's that all about? Does she have nice eyes?

TAMAR:

Actually, she has thick glasses.
Well, her first name is Ilene. "EYE"—lene, Get it?
Sometimes she swears a lot.

RUTH:

She swears when she's talking to you?
I guess we all do sometimes. Do you want to keep seeing her?

TAMAR:

Yeah, I do.

RUTH:

Good, maybe she'll help you stop worrying about your mother.
Cell Phone rings with rap music.
What's that?

TAMAR:

Oh, my cell phone.
While both search for the cell phone, Ruth finds a photograph and stares at it.
Meanwhile, Tamar finds her cell phone.
Hello?
To Ruth.
It's the big "Eye!" She's calling me back!
She exits

RUTH:

Go ahead. I'll find something to do.
Ruth stares at the photograph.

BLACKOUT

ACT 1: SCENE 4

FRONT HALLWAY. HENRY LOOKING TROUBLED

Tamar enters to find Henry smoking a cigarette.

TAMAR:

What are you doing here?
> *Speaks quickly into the phone and hangs up.*

HENRY:

Your mom fell asleep. I really needed the air, and…

TAMAR:

Some space, right?

HENRY:

Sometimes I need room.…

TAMAR:

Tell-tell me about it.

HENRY:.

We have a problem, don't we?

TAMAR:

We had a problem before this-this problem.
Do we, do we have to talk about this now?
I have to talk to my therapist. Then-then I want to be with my grandma,

HENRY:

I'm glad you're in therapy. Anyone I know?

TAMAR:

Duh. You recommended her to me way before you and Mom…

HENRY:

Whew! That's especially good now that your mom…

TAMAR:

Especially??? What?
Is my mom —my mom sick?
Do you know something that she's not telling me?
You're hiding something. What is it?

HENRY:

I've given it away.

TAMAR:

Given WHAT away?
That's—that's not chill!
NOW-now you have to tell me.

HENRY:

She's pregnant. She's going to have my baby.

TAMAR:

Oh. My. God. I KNEW it wasn't the flu. This is TOO weird now!!

HENRY:

 I know. I know.

TAMAR:

Don't you hurt my mother.

HENRY:

I don't want to hurt her, but I'm…

TAMAR:

Yeah you are pretty old.

HENRY:

I have a child a little younger than your mother.

TAMAR:

That's-that's too much to hear. I'd rather just figure this out with Dr. Chapman.

HENRY:

I'm so sorry that I moved here. This is getting rather complicated.

TAMAR:

Were you really my grandfather's friend?

HENRY:

All the way back to college; we used to arm wrestle!

TAMAR:

TMI!! I have enough to…
> *Pause*
Why did you fuck my mom?
> *Sarcastically.*
I look at you and see my grandpa.

HENRY:

I wasn't the initiator.

TAMAR:

I really need to talk to my therapist. I need to go. Now.

She exits. Henry slowly makes his way into the shadows on the other side of the stage.

BLACKOUT

ACT 1: SCENE 5

JUDITH'S BEDROOM.

Judith is groaning on the bed. Chayya tries to sing to her, but no sound comes out.
Judith dials, listens to the ringing and then a recording.

THERAPIST'S VOICE:
If you are a new patient, please make an appointment during office hours. If this is an emergency press one now and leave a short message.

JUDITH:
I need to talk to you immediately. You were right.
> *Ruth knocks on the door.*

I really need to rest. Please Ma, leave me alone.

The door opens a crack to reveal a sliver of light from the hallway. Judith hangs up quickly.

RUTH:
> *Holding the steaming foot bath outside Judith's door.*
Judith it's me.

JUDITH:
How long have you been there?

RUTH:
Not long. Why is everyone asking me this?

JUDITH:
> *Opens the door a crack.*
What have you done with my foot bath?

How did you know what to do with it?

RUTH:

Tamar told me.
Liebkeit, please,
I'm very worried about you.

JUDITH:

Mom, I'm just overworked and overwhelmed.

RUTH:

Liebkeit. Does your new therapist help? I…

JUDITH:

Don't start. I can't bear to see you so concerned. Standing there trying
to take care of me.
It makes me feel guilty.

RUTH:

And that's my fault? Does your therapist tell you that?

JUDITH:

Here we go again.

RUTH:

Why is it always the mother's fault?
What did I ever do to Freud?

JUDITH:

The therapist is a she and I have no energy for this.

RUTH:

I heard you throw up.

JUDITH:

The flu, Ma it's the flu. If you only knew…

RUTH:

Knew what?

JUDITH:

Never mind, you'll never understand.

RUTH:

Try me. You think you're experiencing life for the first time?

JUDITH:

Did you ever work all day and come home as a single mom?

RUTH:

You think it was always a bed of roses for me?
Do you know that your dad and I separated?

JUDITH:

When?
Is that when you got an abortion?

RUTH:

Where did you get such an idea??

JUDITH:

Dad was on NPR talking about your abortion.

RUTH:

He did what?

JUDITH:

When? When did you have it?

RUTH:

Remember your first year at camp?

JUDITH:

I hated it.
I got so homesick I wanted to come home.
You wouldn't let me.

RUTH:

I couldn't take care of you.

JUDITH:

Where was Dad?

RUTH:

On vacation.
He said he needed a vacation. Without me.

JUDITH:

Where did he go?

RUTH:

I don't know. Maybe I didn't want to know,
but I couldn't get in touch with him.

JUDITH:

Neither could I. Even then. So, he wasn't consulting in Europe?

RUTH:

He said he was working in Europe, but it seemed he wanted to stay
on.

JUDITH:

Why?

RUTH:

He never told me.

JUDITH:

Even now?

RUTH:

It hasn't come up again.
He made it clear that he didn't want more children.

JUDITH:

He probably didn't want to take a chance on another girl.

All that arguing when I came back from camp.

RUTH:

Sometimes, it isn't so nice with your father
and sometimes it's very nice.

JUDITH:

But it bothers you.

RUTH:

Not so much anymore.
He's back to being one of my best friends again.
Sometimes that is and sometimes not.

JUDITH:

There goes this idyllic myth about my parents.

RUTH:

Oh yes, myths. You're at that age when myths should die.

JUDITH:

I am not living a myth. I am an independent woman.
I kept my maiden name; I work at helping women…

RUTH:

If you're so liberated, why do you look so enslaved?
You're tired. You're sick.

JUDITH:

Don't you read? Look, here's a whole pile of *Ms.* Magazines.
Please do your homework.

RUTH:

Ms. Magazine? You think I don't know this? That I'm such an old
lady?
Maybe you're an ageist!! Maybe *Ms.* is a feminist myth.
Maybe there's more to this abortion idea than you understand.
Maybe "There are more things in heaven and earth…"

JUDITH:

"… than are dreamt of in your philosophy.
Horatio?"

RUTH:

I remembered it from your Shakespeare course.

JUDITH:

You do learn, don't you?
Someday I'll have to find out what you're up to now…

RUTH:

Maybe I'll crack that myth about mothers being the root of   all
blame.

JUDITH:

Mom! Don't start…
Phone rings
I have to take this.
Talking into her phone.
Hello?

THERAPIST:

Judith? You sounded troubled. I think you should come to the office.

JUDITH:

Mom I need to take this.
Mom, please. This is confidential. It's a client. Please.

RUTH:

You used to tell your mother everything.

JUDITH:

Whispers into the phone as Henry enters and takes off his shirt.
Noticing Ruth, he puts his shirt back on.
I do need to see you immediately.
Mom, please leave so I can talk.
Ruth exits.

HENRY:

Was that who I think? Are you going to do it?
Are you going to get rid of it?

JUDITH:
Covers the phone with her hand; irritated.
This is not an "It!" This is the hope of the future—a global citizen.

HENRY:

To me, a child is not the object of a cause.

JUDITH:

You just don't get me.

HENRY:

Maybe I DO get you. Maybe YOU just want to have a little Jack.

JUDITH:

Henry, please.
Henry. Please. Don't talk to me like that.
Maybe I need some air now.

BLACKOUT

MYTHS AND MS.

INTERMISSION

ACT 2: SCENE 1

DARKENED STAGE

Appearing to be in a daze, Ruth sits alone in a rocking chair, holding a cell phone with a cup of tea nearby. With her feet in the foot bath, Ruth sings, first in Yiddish and then in English in the same melody as the girl hummed earlier.

> *As she sings, Chayya enters.*

RUTH:

Mamelle, Mamelle, zing mir a lieder
Mamelle, Mamelle, der-zeil mir a miceh,
Mamelle, Mamelle, ver bistu yetz as ich daff dir oiych azeh?
Mamma, Mamma, sing me a lullaby,
Mamma, Mamma, tell me a bedtime tale,
Mama Mamma, where are you now that I need you,
Oh, so much.

> *Chayya does a small waltz around Ruth as Ruth dozes off, humming.*
> *Chayya plays the flute, hums the same melody and then sings it very softly.*
> *Ruth startles awake.*

Oiy are you a Dybbuk?

CHAYYA:

You know if I was a Dybbuk you wouldn't be able to see me.

RUTH:

I miss you mama.

CHAYYA:

I know Ruth. That's why I'm here.

RUTH:

Don't you miss me too?

CHAYYA:

It doesn't work that way; I'm here because you called me.

RUTH:

I remember going to sleep with my head on your lap and you would sing to me.
I loved that. Remember your last words to me?

CHAYYA:

I will still sing again.

RUTH:

I wish.

CHAYYA;

I'm glad that my singing is alive in your memory; it helps.

RUTH:

What do you mean?

CHAYYA:

All I know is that I'm here now. You remind me of things undone.

RUTH:

First my daughter blames me and now my mother!
And *you* never even met Freud. Unless that's possible too up there.

CHAYYA:

You'll find out.

RUTH;

Well, maybe Judith could have a baby and you'll come back to me.
Or even Tamar? Eventually.
I dreamt it and dreams are part prophecy; it says so right here.
Pointing to her book.

CHAYYA:

Which part is the truth? And which part is the wish?
More things in this world than you can dream of darling....

RUTH:

Rolls her eyes
That's all I need: A Jewish mother who quotes Hamlet.
Are we really the stuff of dreams Mama? God's dreams?

CHAYYA:

As above so below...

RUTH:

Right from the Zohar. What does all that mean?
How can I make sense of all this haunting? First the baby. And now
you.

CHAYYA:

You always asked good questions. Answers are not so easy.
That's why Jews answer one question with another question.
        Holding both hands out weighing one against the other.
Liebkeit, you have to learn to live with the mystery of life. Of
creation... of...

RUTH:

What does that mean? What about my abortions? Was I wrong to...
Ma? Ma? Where are you going?
Ma! Stay. Please!
        Startles to see Jack opening the door.
        Chayya recedes into the background.
What are you doing here?

JACK:

You just called me.

RUTH:

Are you sure?

JACK:

The cell phone is still in your hand.

RUTH:

I don't remember. Maybe you're a dream.

JACK:

Here, take my hand. I'm not a dream.
  Ruth takes his hand and slowly softens. Then she pulls him nearer.

JACK:

Hello.
Ruthie.
I'm sorry Ruthie.

RUTH:

Sometimes you are so narcissistic!

JACK:

Yes.

RUTH:

And I suppose I have to say I'm really sorry. I'm really, really sorry.

JACK:

This is *our* old merry-go-round.

RUTH:

We did it again.

JACK:

We've worked together; we've fought the good fight together.
We've stayed together through real drama.

RUTH:

I get it: you were trying to get in the lineup for the talk show.
AND, as you were waiting your turn,
cursing the pro-life lady for ranting, I left!

JACK:

That book *Pro-life for the 21ˢᵗ Century* is destroying Roe.
And then you bring up this dream of yours.

RUTH:

But I had just opened the letter.

JACK:

Oh, yeah, a dream unopened; I remember now.
But YOU left *me* this time.
    Scoffing.
Then the house is full of those praying Jews!
Where on earth did you find them?

RUTH:

Oiy. I forgot that the synagogue arranged an extra day of mourning.
In addition to the ones back home.
But I had to come here.
Try to forgive me.
I've forgiven you for worse.

JACK:

Well, if a person asks for forgiveness, I have to, I guess, I have to
               bend.

RUTH:

But you're not bending yet,
    Flirtatiously
are you?

JACK:

No, I'm not bending yet. The cab is still waiting downstairs for me.

RUTH:

Come on. It's time to give up the rant. Isn't it?

JACK:

How have we managed to stay married for this long?

With this dance of ours, this back and forth?

RUTH:

You always say that after a fight, we do get a little excited sometimes.

JACK:

You certainly do and you get me so…so…

RUTH:

Emotional?   For you, emotions are a sin.
For you, you'd rather just take time off and stew…

JACK

You haven't brought that one up in a long time.
We've been over this before.
        Ruth assumes a sitting meditation posture.
There really is no one like you.
We don't get hysterical in my family. We have patience. We wait.
        Silence.

RUTH:

Like what I'm doing now??
        More silence
That was why I married you: your calmness; your lock-step logic.
I would have been a spinning whirlwind without you.

JACK:

Well thank you. Thank you.
You know, after your operation…

RUTH:

After I couldn't have more children?
No sons to teach the right causes to?
You made Judith into a politically correct warrior.

JACK:

OK. OK. We have come a long way haven't we Ruthie?

RUTH:

And you did come back to me when Judith was born.

JACK:

There was never any doubt for me. Does that mean this apology
worked?

RUTH:

Don't push it.
But, maybe, just maybe you could take off your coat?
Maybe you could not talk about my abortion on NPR???

JACK:

The cab is waiting downstairs.
I meant to sneak in quietly.
Tomorrow is that hearing.

RUTH:

To defend the underdog, right?

JACK:

Right.

RUTH:

I got so anxious for Judith. I don't want her to go through what I
went through.
That abortionist didn't even take the cigar out of his mouth.
The nurse walked through the waiting room full of kids like me with
a bloody pan!

JACK:

Wasn't it your choice?

RUTH:

Choice? What is choice when something, a teenage abortion, is
already determined?
The forces around you, above you, beside you,
they determine the choice.
Choice is vastly over-rated and inaccurately named.

JACK:

Well that's a new speech.

RUTH:

That event formed us.

JACK:

I get tired thinking about it now.

RUTH:

It helps me to meditate.
I meditate, so I don't get tired thinking about it.

JACK:

Meditation doesn't relax me. Just looking at you makes me tense.

RUTH:

Looking at the footbath
Okay, I know what you need.

JACK:

Can we drop this for now?
Enough with this spiritualistic stuff.
Can we get back to our daughter?

*Judith opens the door of her room, looks up and down the hall,
slips into the hallway to eavesdrop on her parents.*

RUTH:

Well, we had a nice dinner. Henry cooked it.
Tamar taught me about the delights of foot baths.

JACK:

I have trouble hearing about Henry and his cooking.
He used to cook for the whole co-op.

RUTH:

Drop it Jack. So, you opened a bedroom door and there they were,

screwing!
In Flagrante Delicto! So what? Granted, it WAS a shock, BUT
your temper tantrum was…
Maybe you should think about why she went after Henry…
            Shaking her head…
It's a done deal!
Live with it.
Like me.

JACK:

You're still a pistol!
Now, what is all this present tumult about?

RUTH:

Judith's pregnant. I'm sure of it.
She throws up every morning.

JACK:

I'm still having a hard time talking about stuff.
            Pause.
I guess it's my turn to confess.
Until today, I really thought you were the only one in the world with
crazy dreams.

RUTH:

What?

JACK:

This woman caller described the dreams she had after her abortion.
Apparently, it's some kind of a haunting post-abortion phenomenon.

RUTH:

A part of your body, or what is becoming a body,
has to be remembered somewhere.
It's probably not even fully ensouled yet…

JACK:

There goes all that New Age talk again.
Logic is logic and the mind controls everything.

The mind can talk you into anything, even this this spiritualistic stuff…

RUTH:

Super-imposed. Laughing.
Now *you* sound Buddhist! Those pro-lifers think life occurs at conception.
That's not the issue.
It's when does the soul become embodied in flesh.

JACK:

Who writes this stuff?

RUTH:

This book here describes the forces that bring people together.

JACK:

That would be sex, lusty sex.
We lusted after each other, and, in our case, we turned that spark into love.
I didn't know what to do with my life then.

RUTH:

You certainly do know now. And you did stand by me once; I can't forget that.
That's the one you talked about on NPR? Not the one I did solo?
It was quite an experience. All that fear.   All that anxiety.

Judith recoils in agony.

JACK:

That was then and this is now.

RUTH:

I keep trying to remember that, but Judith's on my mind.

JACK:

What about her?

RUTH:

Judith is very, very tired. She had a confidential call.

Judith, now bent in anxiety, comes closer to Tamar's bedroom door.

JACK:

Well, we did something right. I'm so proud of her for doing that
              work,
counseling young women and men in crisis.

RUTH:

You better slip out before she gets up.

JACK:

I'm the sorry one now. I <u>must</u> go.
              Takes a brief sip of her tea.
Please keep me posted.

*Judith quickly tiptoes past them, then slips by their door, down the hallway,
and out the front door.*

Chayya steps out from the wings and follows her.

ACT 2: SCENE 2

THE FRONT PORCH

A door slams from inside the house.

   Henry hears a voice saying, "Please keep me posted."

   Jack slams the outer door. Judith peeks back to listen to Henry. Jack is texting a message and nearly collides with Henry who plants himself in Jack's path.

Judith weeps silently from her hiding place.

JACK:

What the F...

HENRY:

I believe that's "W." "T." "F" if you are texting...

JACK:

What the fuck are you doing here???

HENRY:

I might ask you the same question.

JACK:

I came to see my wife!!

HENRY:

Not your daughter? She's the one that needs you.

JACK:

Where are you coming from? You betrayed me with my own daughter!

HENRY:

Did you ever wonder why she came to me and not you?

JACK:

What are you talking about?

HENRY:

What were you thinking? Too busy to talk to your own daughter.
Too busy with work, with your many causes.
The only time you talked was about policy, politics, and
demonstrations

JACK:

What? Oh, my god!

HENRY:

That's the god you don't believe in?

JACK:

Jeez don't be a wise ass!
  Pause. He begins to arm wrestle Henry.
Remember this.

HENRY:

I remember always winning.

They continue for a time until both men are winded and exhausted.

JACK:

You didn't win that time.

HENRY:

Nor did you.
  Pause
So what happened with the first guy? Her husband?

JACK:

That kid was like a son to me...

HENRY:

The son you wanted Judith to be?
When's the last time you actually looked at her,
Listened to what was on her mind?
She's a woman who doesn't appreciate being lectured at.

JACK:

Now you've gone too far.

More arm wrestling. Jack pushes Henry who stumbles, falls, gets injured, and realizes he's bleeding.

Jeez Henry. You're diabetic; you have to take care of that.

HENRY:

You are hopeless. I do have to take care of this.
> *Exits into the house.*

Judith comes out of the shadows shaking and crying, finally able to release her anguish.
Jack turns aghast, then he holds her while she weeps for a time, sometimes retching.

JACK:

Your mother did that when she was pregnant with you.
I used to tell her to put her hands on my shoulders, look at me, and breathe.
We would breathe together until she stopped.
> *Pause.*
Judith, what did I do to you?

JUDITH:

Dad stop being weird. You didn't do this to me. Henry did.
It's even weirder that an abortion counsellor is on her way to have an abortion.

JACK:

What's even weirder is that your mom…

Stops.

JUDITH:

I know about mom's abortion and your absence. I finally got the whole story from her.

JACK:

How did you get that out of her?

JUDITH:

Next time you say personal stuff on the radio, you should consider who else is listening.

JACK:

I never even thought…

JUDITH:

I know. You never think about the repercussions of the stuff that you do.

JACK:

Like making you into, what did Mom call it, a politically correct warrior woman?

JUDITH:

Duh! I could never match up. Why didn't you love me for ME?
Jack staggers.
Look at me. Look at me.
Breathe.
Breathe with me.

JACK:

I almost…I was dreaming that I was in court.
That I needed a lawyer!
Wait.
Pause.
You just said that you are going to have an abortion?
I could have had a grandson?

JUDITH:

It's not about you. It's about me.

JACK:

What am I supposed to do now?

JUDITH:

Let me go and have an abortion.

JACK:

Alone? Your mother was alone!
Maybe that's why I was just on trial.

JUDITH:

One more time Dad: this is not about you or your trial. Please.

JACK:

You can't go alone!!
I won't let you.

JUDITH:

Now what? Are you going to call Mom, or Henry, or even Tamar?

JACK:

I'm going with you.

JUDITH:

Dad, you just almost fainted. How…

JACK:

Super-imposed
I will not faint at this.
I won't go to my grave not having taken care of my daughter.
I failed your mother, I won't fail you.

BLACKOUT

ACT 2: SCENE 3

JUDITH'S KITCHEN NEXT MORNING

With her feet in the footbath, Ruth is looking at a picture of her mother and herself.

Sniffling, she rocks herself in the chair, cradling the picture. She hums and sings first in Yiddish and then in English. When the door opens she quickly takes up a book, slips the picture into it, and appears to read. Chayya is whiter than before. Judith enters looking pale and exhausted. She spent the night at the clinic.

JUDITH:

Hi mom.

RUTH:

Judith, where have you been? I've been so worried.

JUDITH:

Yeah, I had to go grocery shopping, but the line was too long so I left and did a bunch of other errands.

RUTH:

Didn't you go shopping yesterday?

JUDITH:

I forgot a few things. I was stuck in traffic for an hour, crawling
          along, not moving.
I think there was an accident or something from the weather.

RUTH:

You don't look so good Judith.

JUDITH:

I am tired. I think I've been coming down with something for a long time.

RUTH:
Well, something is not right. Maybe you want your footbath back?

JUDITH:
Maybe.

RUTH:
I just wonder: do you and Henry ever use it together?

JUDITH:
Well, aren't we nosy? I never asked you much about stuff with Dad?
Tamar and I were planning on using it together.
Glances at the picture.
This looks like Tamar and a much younger you.

RUTH:
No that's my mother and me. I do look like Tamar there, don't I?

JUDITH:
What's going on Mom?

RUTH:
I accused Dad of hiding this picture from me and it turned up on
                    Tamar's worktable.
She probably needed it for her family portraits project.

JUDITH:
I didn't even know that she had such a project.

RUTH:
Judith, you never told me anything when you were her age.

JUDITH:
It was always Bubby who knew me.

RUTH:
Well that's how the generational thing works I guess.

JUDITH:

Where is Tamar now?

RUTH:

Oh, I think she went to talk to her therapist.

JUDITH:

Do you know about her hair? Is it still fuchsia?

RUTH:

I think she said purple, maybe magenta. I try not to be intrusive.
I remember you at her age.

JUDITH:

And I remember you and that time also!
But what I don't remember is what Dad recalled on that talk show!
Why didn't you ever tell me?

RUTH:

About what?

JUDITH:

About what happened before I was born. Dad talked about your
abortion.

RUTH:

What good would it do for a young child to know a thing like that?

JUDITH:

Ok, I can understand why you didn't tell me then. But now?

RUTH:

Do we talk about anything now? You have no idea about me.

JUDITH:

And you seem to have no idea about me now.

RUTH:

WHY do you think I came? I'm here because Tamar was worried.

JUDITH:

What?

RUTH:

She and I talk from time to time. These things skip a generation sometimes.

JUDITH:

Are you saying that I don't have a connection with my own daughter?

RUTH:

Now you're insulted? Isn't that what you used to tell me?
Tamar was worried because you throw up every morning.
She can hear you. I don't believe it's the flu.

JUDITH:

YOU had an abortion. Isn't it timely that I learned about it now?

RUTH:

What about now?

JUDITH:

I just came from — today — I just came from — I just had an abortion.

RUTH:

I knew it! You went alone? I knew something was up.
But Liebkeit, you went alone. All by yourself!

JUDITH:

I wasn't alone. Dad came with me.

RUTH:

I knew he had it in him!

JUDITH:

I thought you'd be surprised after…

RUTH:

…After going it alone to…?

JUDITH:

Well, Yeah!

RUTH:

I told my supervisor about it, and she asked me, "Do you think he's capable of change?"

JUDITH:

Resigned
And you said "yes!"

RUTH:

I didn't answer, but now I would say "yes." Young love images the future your love can be.

JUDITH:

Alright! Enough.

RUTH:

Judith, you don't understand that he had to fail me to learn to be with you. Your father's brilliance froze his emotions. When his Uncle Ted lied about his age to fight the Nazis, his favorite uncle never came back. So your father fixated on righting all the wrongs.

JUDITH:

I know this family story only partially, but you are saying now that Dad relied on his head and imprisoned his heart because…wow. So social action became his religion.

RUTH:

And yours too!
Long silence while Judith absorbs this idea.

JUDITH:

Dad mentioned your recurrent dream. There's help for things like that now.

RUTH:

My parents—Oiy, my parents—I couldn't tell them.
They would die!

JUDITH:

It's different now, Ok?

RUTH:

There was another abortion.
When I was younger and Dad was a senior camp counselor.
The abortionist never even took the cigar out of his mouth!
    Pause.
Liebkeit, I would have taken your baby. I would have raised him. Or her.

JUDITH:

That would end those recurrent dreams Mom?

RUTH:

We weren't sure we had a future together.

JUDITH:

I'm not sure about my future.

RUTH:

What about Tamar's future?
What about the effect of all this on her?

JUDITH:

Are you suggesting that Tamar is pregnant?

RUTH:

I never even thought of that.

JUDITH:

You could have been honest with me.

RUTH:

Do you think I wanted you to know that I broke the law?
What are you going to tell Tamar?

JUDITH:

It's not against the law now. I may not even tell Tamar.

RUTH:

See! What was I supposed to do?
"Judith, I'm coming over for lunch. I have to tell you about the sibling you might have had."

JUDITH:

I just wish I'd known. We could have been different together.
Anyway, now you are the first one to know.

RUTH:

Really? Henry doesn't know?   Does he want this baby?

JUDITH:

It doesn't matter anymore.

RUTH:

It would be fair to tell him.
He's not ready for any of this.

JUDITH:

It's not fair to me.
I'm the one who wanted a son,
a cosmopolitan citizen of the world.

RUTH:

You'd have a child to support a cause?

JUDITH:

I really don't want to talk about it now.

RUTH:

So, you don't want to talk about your dilemma
but you want me to talk about mine.
You wouldn't be interested in your old mother's gory dreams.

JUDITH:

What are you talking about?

RUTH:

The pieces of the fetus reforming into a baby.
That baby would be older than you.
I keep seeing the face.

JUDITH:

I know about this. I'm a social worker. Many of my clients dream
about aborted fetuses.
I dream more since I conceived.
The fetus was always running after me.

RUTH:

I think that will stop now.

JUDITH:

How do you know that? Anyway, life of the fetus hasn't really started
yet.

RUTH:

Real life, the life of the spirit doesn't just start and it doesn't end.
It's when does that soul become embodied. No one knows that.

JUDITH:

I'm sure Dad thinks this is nonsense.

RUTH:

He thinks that I'm hysterical.

JUDITH:

We do get over everything don't we Mom? Eventually.

Henry and I came together for the wrong reasons.

RUTH:

I wish you hadn't done it.
I would have taken the baby.

JUDITH:

I shouldn't have told you. You can't make up for your regrets this way
Mom.

RUTH:

Really, I would've taken the baby.

JUDITH:

Stop redacting please. I really need to be alone. Please.

RUTH:

Liebkeit, I'm so sorry Liebkeit.

JUDITH:

Don't do this now.

RUTH:

I'm a failure. I'm a total failure with my abortion and I'm a total
failure with you.

JUDITH:

Mom, I can't deal with this. I've had a hard day.

RUTH:

OK. I'll go home.
What about Tamar?

JUDITH:

She'll be alright. She has a good therapist.

RUTH:

Do you have enough food?

JUDITH:

Yes, mom.

RUTH:

Judith?
> *Pause.*

Can I take the footbath?

JUDITH:

Yeah, fine, sure just take it.

RUTH:

Are you sure?

JUDITH:

Please, just take it and go. I don't care. I need to lie down
> *Ruth picks up the footbath, but trips, spilling the water all over the floor.*

RUTH:

I'll clean it up. Look, I'm wiping the floor.
> *Wiping the floor. She slowly gets up holding her back.*

Judith, can we have a goodnight hug?

JUDITH:

Our old bedtime ritual? OK.
> *Delivers a reluctant hug.*

Ruth exits.

Henry! Henry! Where are you?

BLACKOUT

ACT 2: SCENE 4

THE HALLWAY.

TAMAR:

I hate bumping into you in the hall.
Wait.
Why are you bleeding?

HENRY:

Your grandfather bested me.

TAMAR:

Good for gr-grandpa!
Did you play that aging diabetic card again?

> *Henry is visibly hurt.*

HENRY:

I didn't realize it was a card to play.
Wow. Maybe Judith is with me out of sympathy...

TAMAR:

You're being dramatic.
> *Changes her tone as she realizes Henry is indeed wounded.*
Henry, remember when you were our kind uncle,
the uncle that listened to us after grandpa finished his lecture on the
news?

HENRY:

Maybe Judith is getting tired of this May-September affair.

TAMAR:

I don't know what that is.

HENRY:

It's an old fashioned way of describing a couple with a huge age difference.

TAMAR:

I liked it better when you were our understanding uncle; it was a welcome relief.

Her phone rings and she reads a text.

HENRY:

Like "good cop/bad cop," only now the good cop went bad.

TAMAR:

You said that, I didn't.

HENRY:

You're not stuttering.

TAMAR:

Knowing I'm right about this, makes m-me…

HENRY:

Hmpf. Naming a thing calls for a relapse.
What's wrong?
Talk to me.

TAMAR:

I-I used to l-love talking to you.

HENRY:

And now… can you…

TAMAR:

Showing him the text.
It's my boyfriend.

HENRY:

Josh? Why is that upsetting you?

TAMAR:

I'm with Josh, or I should be with Josh because…

HENRY:

Which means what…?

TAMAR:

I missed my period, and he's…
> *Covers her mouth; she's said too much.*

HENRY:

So you… ?

TAMAR:

This is your old "finish the sentence" technique?

HENRY:

Sometimes it works or it did in the past.

TAMAR:

I'm not-not ready to f-finish the sentence yet.

HENRY:

As you wish.

TAMAR:

Is this how you seduced my mother?

HENRY:

I knew you were bright, but I didn't think you were this….
Tamar, you should talk to Dr. Chapman about all this.

TAMAR:

Enough flattery. About my mom, you got her to open up and then…
Now you want to…

HENRY:

Soon, I think I may be ready to finish that sentence.

TAMAR:

Then do it. Be my Uncle Henry again.

HENRY:

It's still an incomplete sentence.

TAMAR:

We both have things to complete.
 Returns to her text message and begins texting.

JUDITH:

 Calls loudly from the other room.
HENRY? HENRY! Where are you?

HENRY:

I should go now.

They exit in different directions.

BLACKOUT

ACT 2 SCENE 5

TAMAR'S BEDROOM

Tamar is on the phone with her therapist.

TAMAR:
Speaking into her phone.
I'm freaking out Dr. Chapman. I think I'm pregnant.
What should I....
Knocking at the door.
It must be my grandmother. No one knocks on my door here.

RUTH:
Enters with Chayya.
I must pack because I'm going. Your mother doesn't want me here.

TAMAR:
I have to hang up.
Hangs up the phone .

RUTH:
I'll just keep packing and you can keep talking.
Ruth keeps packing and starts cleaning up Tamar's room.

TAMAR:
Grandma, you don't have to clean my room. No one does that here.

RUTH:
I think I'm crowding your mother.

TAMAR:
What do you mean?
We have enough room here.

RUTH:

I think it's just better if I just go.

TAMAR:

It's not better for me if you leave.
When you're here, I don't have those dreams.

RUTH:

Oh, Mama!
Looks up at the ceiling.
I think I'm in the way here.

TAMAR:

That's not fair!
What about me?

RUTH:

It's almost the end of the semester.
Maybe you could come to me to sleep over again?

TAMAR:

Just like when I was little.

RUTH:

Excited
You want to come and see us then?

TAMAR:

Yeah, it would be nice to get a break from here.

RUTH:

Well, if I bring you a little cheer, then maybe my life is worth
something.

TAMAR:

Grandma, don't say that. The whole family depends on you.

RUTH:

Well, maybe.

Just tell me one thing: do you like Henry?

TAMAR:

I liked him better when I thought of him as an uncle.

RUTH:

Poor man, he's really not equipped for this.
  Pause.
So, you'll come for a visit?

TAMAR:

I really want to grandma. I really want to.

BLACKOUT

ACT 2 SCENE 6

JACK AND RUTH'S LIVING ROOM.

Ruth & Jack, with their feet in the footbath, are both draped in the bedsheet from Scene 1.

RUTH:
See, Jack, it's not so bad.
> *Playfully touches Jack in the footbath. A courting footsies game*
continues.

JACK:
I'm getting the hang of it.
> *Shyly*
I do have trouble with this.
Ruth, stop coaching me, that makes me want to pull out.

RUTH:
Did you see me doing any coaching?

JACK:
We've been married a long time. I can tell when you are coaching.
I have learned a few things about you.

RUTH:
How about me? Have I learned anything about you?

JACK:
Maybe, but you don't act on it as often as I'd like.

RUTH:
I already apologized.
I may be done apologizing if you don't watch out.

JACK:

Why on earth did you have to go traipsing over there on a hunch?
You Jewish Mothers are so nosy and over-protective.

RUTH:

You seemed to like it at one time. Why are you bringing this up now?

JACK:

Maybe I'm still upset.
Henry meant so much to me.

RUTH:

Remember when you visited Ma in that nursing home?
When the door to her room was held closed by a chair.

JACK:

Begins laughing and can't seem to stop.
I thought something was wrong. So, I struggled to open that door and
there's your mother in bed with her boyfriend.

RUTH:

And she says "Jack, how nice to see you!"
They both laugh.

JACK:

I never knew your mother until that moment.

RUTH:

I was embarrassed for years about it until she told me all those stories
about Emma
Goldman and free love. Ma always said, "Emma had a good time in
life."

Chayya appears and enjoys what she observes here.

JACK:

Is that where our daughter gets it from?

RUTH:

I'm proud of what you did for her. But how did you know?

JACK:

Judith told me. She always tells me when it's important.
Like the time she eloped.
Like the time he left her.
We just had a little hiatus.

RUTH:

So, what else did she say?

JACK:

She let me have it for…a lot of things.
She wanted to know if I was disappointed.
She wanted to know about you. About your abortion…
Were you afraid? How did I act?
So, I told her.

RUTH:

And?

JACK:

She talked about Henry.

RUTH:

What is she going to do?

JACK:

What her gut tells her to do.

RUTH:

Have you ever thought what it would be like if there was another
child now? A son?

JACK:

Sometimes.

They are getting cozier in the footbath and playing with the sheet that surrounds them. Little by little, they get closer.

RUTH:

It's been a long time, hasn't it? I'm sorry I was so insistent.

JACK:

That was then. I was insistent also.
Let's just be together in this moment now.
 More smooching.
 Phone rings.
Let it ring babe. It's been a long time.

RUTH:

 Looks at caller I.D.
But it's Judith!

JACK:

She's a big girl. Ruthie, she's an adult. We'll call her later.

RUTH:

But I'm a Jewish mother who puts her children first!

JACK:

Time to learn something new. Children will always blame their
    parents for everything
anyway. Gratitude comes after we die.
 Chayya grimaces.
 Jack begins to kiss Ruth.

The doorbell rings

JACK:

We could lay low.

RUTH:

Our car is in the driveway.

JACK:

Where's the towel?

Persistent knocking, then banging on the door followed by a muffled voice.

RUTH:

I forgot the towel!
        Jumps up with wet feet and opens the front door still draped in the sheet.

Holding a full backpack, Tamar stands in the doorway.

Chayya's white face assumes more color as she smiles.

BLACKOUT

END OF PLAY

OTHER
ANAPHORA LITERARY
PRESS TITLES

PLJ: Interviews with Gene Ambaum and Corban Addison: VII:3, Fall 2015
Editor: Anna Faktorovich

Architecture of Being
By: Bruce Colbert

The Encyclopedic Philosophy of Michel Serres
By: Keith Moser

Forever Gentleman
By: Roland Colton

Janet Yellen
By: Marie Bussing-Burks

Diseases, Disorders, and Diagnoses of Historical Individuals
By: William J. Maloney

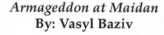

Armageddon at Maidan
By: Vasyl Baziv

Vovochka
By: Alexander J. Motyl

CPSIA information can be obtained
at www.ICGtesting.com
Printed in the USA
BVOW09s0920091017

496927BV00001B/2/P